Book 1

Fortran Crash Course

By: PG WIZARD BOOKS

Book 2

XML

By: PG WIZARD BOOKS

Book 1

Fortran Crash Course

By: PG WIZARD BOOKS

Step By Step Guide To Mastering Fortran Programming!

Fortran Crash Course: Step By Step Guide To Mastering Fortran
Programming!

Fortran Crash Course: Step By Step Guide To Mastering Fortran
Programming!

Table of Contents

Introduction

Fortran Crash Course: Step By Step Guide To Mastering Fortran
Programming!

Introduction

Many beginners to coding worry that they are not going to be able to learn how to work with a new coding language. They feel that it is going to be too difficult to learn the language and that they will either not be able to do some of the programming that they want or that they just won't understand what is being said in the information. But when it comes to working with Fortran, you will find that learning how to code is a simple process.

In this guidebook, we are going to start out by talking about some of the information that comes with Fortran. We will also work on the first code for this language and discuss all the different parts that are going to be found inside of your code. This is a simple introduction to help you get some practice with writing your own code and ensures that you are able to get into some of the more complex situations that we will discuss later on.

Once we have these basics down, we are going to move on to some of the other things that you are able to do when it comes to working on your code in Fortran. We will take a look at writing some of your own loop statements, what strings and arrays are, working with conditional statements, and so much more. Even as a beginner, you will be able to use these options in order to make a really strong code and program as you want it.

When you are ready to get into coding and want to make sure that you are designing something that is strong and will work the way that you want, Fortran is one of the best coding languages to help you learn how to get it done. Make sure to use this guidebook to help you to get the basics to work with Fortran for all your coding needs.

Chapter 1: Learning the Basics of Fortran

As a beginner, you may have times that you are worried that a new coding language will be too hard for you to learn. You want to make your own programs, learn how to work in different operating systems, or have another goal that you would like to accomplish, but you worry that it is going to be too much work for you to accomplish because it will be too hard to do. But when it comes to learning how to work with Fortran (which is basically a contraction of Formula Translation), you are working with a great language that is designed for beginners, even for those that have no experience in coding before.

Fortran is considered one of the oldest programming languages that you can use and this can be a benefit as well as an issue. It is beneficial because you will be able to find this language anywhere that you want to look and the compiler, as well as the other add-ons, are all going to be free. It is a coding language that many scientists and engineers like to use because of all the functions that are built in and the fact that it is easily used with mathematical constructs. There are also many other things that you are able to do with this coding language, and since it is one of the oldest options around, you are sure to find lots of help and answers to ensure that you get the project done right.

What will I need to get started?

When you are ready to get started with Fortran, you will need to bring out a new text editor. There are several of these that are available, and you can choose the one that works for you. You need this because it allows you to out the codes so that the compiler, which you will need next, will be able to read out what you are doing and tell the computer how to behave. You are not able to use a word processor for this because these kinds of applications are not going to save files in plain text, which is required to make the compiler do its job.

Next on the list is the compiler. There are many options out there and most of them are going to be free as well so you can download these and not have to worry about adding in costs. Basically the compiler is going to take the words that you have written in the text editor and then change them around into something that the computer is actually able to read. You will just need to save your code and then the compiler will be able to execute it.

Fortran Crash Course: Step By Step Guide To Mastering Fortran Programming!

Some people find that working with an Integrated Development Environment, or IDE, is a great way to help make this a lot easier. This IDE is going to work similar to the text editor and the compiler in one so it saves you some time, especially when it comes to troubleshooting the written code. For those who are working on Windows computers, the IDE is really a good idea because it has an interface that is easy to sue and similar to what you are used to seeing on the Windows computer.

As mentioned, you could just use the text editor and the compiler, but the IDE does make it a bit easier to write your code. These combine both of the other two products in one and it is able to understand syntaxes of the code easily. In fact, it is going to be able to catch some of the errors that come up in the code as you are typing, saving a lot of time and accidents in the process.

The benefits of using Fortran for your coding

There are so many reasons why you may want to consider using Fortran as your coding language of choice. Whether you are looking to use it on the side as another coding language to master or this is one of the first coding languages that you are going to work with, the benefits of choosing this one are amazing. Some of the reasons that you would want to work with the Fortran coding language include:

- Easy to use: Fortran was designed for the beginner to learn how to use it. It is a simple language to work with and after looking at some of the codes in this book, you are sure to see that it is easy enough to learn how to work with.
- Has been around for a long time: Fortran is one of the first coding languages that came available for coders to use in their homes. This is a good thing because it is simplistic and easy to use. We are going to work on a few different codes inside of this guidebook and you will find that most of them are pretty straight forward and easy to write, even if you are a beginner. While some people feel that the fact that Fortran has been around for so long is a bad thing, it can mean so many good things for helping you to get the very best when working in coding.

- Great for the scientific community: this is a language that anyone is able to use for their own needs, but it is specifically important when it comes to the scientific community. If you have an occupation that is in this field, you will find that it is a good idea to learn how to use the Fortran code.
- Lots of programs still use it: even though this is an older coding language that you can use, there are still a lot of programs that use it. This means that you will have plenty of chances to use this programming language and to get some more practice.
- Can be modified for other languages: Fortran is one of the earliest coding languages that is out there so it has had many adaptations over the years. This means that there are versions that you are able to use and combine with some of your other programming languages. This makes it easier to do some of the more powerful things that you want to do with your coding.
- It is free: all the stuff that you need for Fortran, from the software itself to the IDE that you want to use with it, is all free to use. This makes it easier for everyone to use this language because you won't have to worry about all the costs that are associated with it.
- Has a big community: when it comes to using a brand new language, you want to make sure that you have a community that is able to answer your questions and make sure that you going on the right track. Since Fortran has been around for so long, there are many people who know how to use this and can be there to help you out.

There are many benefits to using the Fortran coding language. While some people prefer to go with another option that is easier or newer to use, there are still many people who want to work with Fortran because it is one of the first. It is a simplistic language to learn how to use even as a beginner, and it is able to get a lot of the coding and programming done that you would like. If you are looking for a coding language that is pretty easy to work with and is meant for beginners, you won't go wrong when choosing Fortran.

How to test my first code

Fortran Crash Course: Step By Step Guide To Mastering Fortran
Programming!

Now that we have spent some time talking about the things that you need to get started with the Fortran coding, it is time to test out one of our first codes. Once you have taken the time to install the IDE that you would like to use, it is time to double click on the icon so that the programming environment is going to open up. You can then create a brand new file but keep in mind that you may need to select on a Fortran file when you do this, just in case the IDE that you picked is able to read more than one language. So you will need to give it the extension of .f95 rather than of .txt so that you are able to compile these statements a bit later on.

One thing to keep in mind is that there are some other extensions that you are able to use when it comes to Fortran including .FOR, .F, and FPP. These extensions are going to tell the compiler was standards you are following with the work you do so make sure that you pick the one that you want and stick with it. You can experiment a bit to figure out which one you want to use.

So once you are done picking out the extension that you would like to use (we are going to stick with the .f95 one for now), we are going to need to type out the following code to get started:

program mytest

!this is a test

Print *, 'This is an output test'

end program mytest

After we have taken the time to type out this bit of code, it is time to execute it inside of the IDE. Your compiler will then go through and double check the parts of the code, looking to see if you have made any errors in the code before trying to run it. If there are any errors that show up, the IDE will let you know and ask you to fix it. If there aren't any troubles with the code, the compiler is going to generate and then execute the file. Basically, with this one you are going to find that the words "This is an output test" will show up on the screen if you typed it in the right way.

Breaking down this code

Now that we have taken some time to write our own code, it is time to break it down to make a bit more sense. Like a lot of the other coding languages that are out there, the Fortran language is going to take care of the different lines of the code, which are called statements, and then decide what it is going to do with each of them. So in the first line, the program is going to state the name of the program that you are trying to work with.

Then moving on to the second line, you are working with a comment. This basically means that you are writing a little note for yourself or for the other programmers that are taking a look at the code. The compiler knows that it shouldn't execute the comment since this is just a little note. You can add in as many comments as you would like inside of the code to describe what the different parts are going to do.

The third line of the code is the output command that is going to tell the compiler what it is supposed to display on the screen. It is going to show up in a single quote. You can make this statement as long or short as you would like, just make sure that you are using the right options with it. And then in the last line, the statement is terminating, or ending, the program that you just write.

Now, this is a pretty basic option that we are working on and only has four lines. There are many options that you are able to do with Fortran that will use more lines to get it done depending on the things that you are doing inside the code. There are also a few versions of Fortran that will have the code look a bit different. Basically all of them need to have the four same parts including the program name, the output statements (you may have more than one of these in some cases), end of program, and comments if you need them.

Making sure that you have all the right parts in place in order to write the code is important to helping the compiler to work with you on creating the code. And while there are many different data types that you are able to use, as we will discuss as we go on in this guidebook, they can be as simple or as difficult as you need to make the code work.

Chapter 2: Working on Loops in Fortran

When you are working on writing your own code inside of Fortran, you need to understand how to work with loops. There are many different times when you will want the code to keep repeating something, or do a specific action more than once. With the most basic form of your code, you would need to write this part of the code over and over again. Now, if you just want the code to repeat a few times, this may not seem like such a big deal, but what happens when you want to write out the code 100 times? Rewriting the same part 100 times can get tiring and old pretty quickly.

But with loops, you are able to tell the compiler to repeat the same steps until the conditions are no longer true. This could be five times and it could be 1000 times, but you would just need to write out a few lines of code to make this happen. Rather than having to write out the same instructions over and over again, you are able to set up the loop to do the same functions over and over again.

There are several different components that are going to be found inside of a loop to make sure that it is going to work. The main components include:

- Step: this component is going to tell the compiler that the procedure will need to be repeated at least once.
- Start: this is going to tell the compiler that it is at the beginning of your loop.
- Stop: this is going to tell the compiler that it is at the end of your loop.
- Var: this is a variable. It is in charge of telling the compiler how many times that you would need to have your code repeated.

How do these loops work?

Loops are going to begin when you set the start and then you define the var. they will explore what concept you are working with inside the var and decide when the conditions have no longer been met so this will all start. As soon as your statement is executed once, the amount to the var is going to go up by one so that you don't end up in an endless loop. So, if you want to make a table that goes from one to ten, the var would start at one and

then each time it goes up by one until it reaches ten. Let's take a look at a
sample code that shows how the loop function is going to work:

```
program loop_factorial

implicit none


        !definition of variables

        Integer::xfact=1

        Integer::x


        !computations of factorials

        Do x=1, 15

                Xfact=xfact*1

                Write*, x, xfact

        End do

End program loop_factorial
```

This one is a bit longer than what we are used to with the other code we
wrote, but it does show how the loop is going to work for you. This one is
going to make sure that the variable will keep going up by one each time
that you work with it, helping to keep things organized and to ensure that
you don't end up in an endless loop. If you do end up with a loop that
doesn't have a stop point, you are going to get stuck inside of the code and
have trouble getting out without closing the whole program.

There are a few different types of loops that you are able to work with.
Some are going to check the conditions the statement before
determining whether or not to run the loop. If the conditions are not true
from the beginning, you are not going to get the loop to run at all and it is
going to head on to the next part of the code. This is known as the for loop.
And then the do while loop is going to run the loop at least one time, and
then run check the options to see if it meets the condition. The choice can
be the same, but it does depend on whether you want the code to run one
time or it doesn't matter.

The loop is one of the best things that you can work with when trying to make your code look nice and organized when on Fortran. You will be able to tell the loop how many times you would like it to run through the program, just using a few lines rather than rewriting the code all of the time. This is an efficient way to work inside of your code and ensures that the code is still able to work properly.

Chapter 3: Working with Strings and Arrays

When you are working with Fortran, you will find that strings and arrays are great ways to help keep the code organized. There are certain ways that you will be able to work with these in order to get them to execute inside of the code properly. In this chapter, we are going to spend some time talking about what strings and arrays are and how you would be able to work with them inside your code.

What are strings?

Inside of the Fortran code, all characters are going to be seen as one of two elements. They are seen as either single characters or contiguous strings. So what is the difference between them? With a contiguous string, you will notice that their length for syntax declaration is going to be passed, they will allow you to do notations on the substring, they won't allow you to do notation on arrays, they can contain descriptors if needed, and in some cases there are going to be hidden arguments inside.

When you want to declare a string inside of Fortran, you are going to use rules that are similar to declaring some of the other variables. So in order to do this, you would use the following option (we are giving the string an assignment of 10):

specifier :: variable_name

character(len=10)::name

Now in addition to working on the string, you will be able to work on substrings, which are basically just smaller parts of the string. They are going to be any part of the program that is executed and you are able to extract them if you wish. For example, if you have a long string that is several sentences long, you could work on a substring and just take out a few of the words to make it easier to read if you want. Here is an example of how you would be able to take out substrings from the string inside the code:

```
program string_concatenation

implicit non


      character (len=5) :: name

      character (len=50) :: announcement

      character (len=50) :: message


      name = 'Dana Caulfield'

      announcement = 'This is'

      message = 'I would like to give you a warm welcome to Prescott
Academy!'


print *, announcement, name

print * , message

end program string_concatenation
```

With this option you are going to get the message "This is Dana Caulfield. I would like to give you a warm welcome to Prescott Academy!" You are able to choose how much of the message you would like to do and you can keep it all on one line or on more than one. For example, you could choose to just have "This is Dana Caulfield" show up on the screen if you would like. This gives you some options to have a longer phrase there if you would like while also keeping it so that you get smaller patches as well.

Concatenation

Another thing that we are going to take a look at when working inside of Fortran is known as concatenation. You are going to notice that it will use the (//) symbol in order to show that this is inside the code. The concatenation property is the one that describes which programs are able to link back to each other. Because of these connections that are established, the main goal is to either draw attention over to another branch in the program, or to make sure that the framework is solid. In some cases the links are going to be for two separate programs, but often the subjects are going to be single elements.

You can also work with a process that is known as trimming. This is when you want to cut out parts of the line that are not necessary so that you get the right result to show up. Since there can often be elements inside the program that aren't needed and are known as trailing blanks, the process of trimming is going to help to get rid of some of this clutter so that you are able to just use the portions that are needed. It also helps your compiler to be able to read through the code faster.

There are a lot of things that you are able to do with the strings inside of your projects and you will be able to mess around with them a bit to get the strings to work out the way that you want. But using concatenation and trimming will help to ensure that you are using the strings in the proper manner.

Arrays

Arrays are another important part of working on your code. They are going to be in charge of storing information, such as variables and characters, that are similar. If the piles of data aren't stored in the proper way, it is going to be really hard for the computer to be able to interpret them. However, when you use the arrays properly to put this information in the right places, the compiler is going to have a better chance at running the program and the functions will be executed in the proper way. Some of the things that you should remember about arrays to make it easier include:

- If you would like to specify the individual elements, you are going to need to address them using the subscripts. The first element is going to have the subscript of 1.
- If you see the term "extent' it is going to describe the elements that are along a dimension. Keep in mind that this is a numerical value.
- On the other hand, if you see the term rank, it is going to describe the dimensions that they have, using a numerical value as well.
- When you see the term "size" this is going to describe the elements that the array has, using numerical values again.
- The shape of the array is going to consist of elements.
- They are going to be declared with the attribute of dimension.

- They are going to be linked to memory locations that are contiguous.

There are two types of arrays that you are able to find inside of the Fortran language. The one-dimensional arrays are the ones that will serve as vectors while the two-dimensional arrays are the ones that will serve as the matrices.

Now that we know a little bit more about arrays, it is time to understand how you are going to be able to declare the arrays. Luckily this is a process that is pretty easy to complete. The rule is to specify the dimension that you desire, and then the compiler will be able to take a look at the elements that are involved and determine if they are an integer or real. For example, if you want to declare an array that is the Caulfield Lair and you want to give it seven elements, you would use the following code to make it happen:

real, dimension (7) :: Caulfield Lair.

Now you can also choose to declare an array that is two dimensional. Let's say that we are still using the example of Caulfield Lair from above, but we are going to make it so that the elements are 7 by 7. To do this, we are going to use the following syntax:

integer, dimension (7, 7) :: Caulfield Lair.

If you would like to make sure that you are assigning the right values to your arrays, you will find that the process is pretty simple. You just need to work on the array and then enter in the amount that you would like to use. You do have some choices when it comes to doing this because you can either do it on a single element that you want to change or you can work it out on the whole array. Let's take a look at an example of how this would work. Let's say that we want to add in the value of 3 to all of the elements would need the following code:

```
do I = 1, 7

        Caulfield Lair = i*3.0
```

17

end program do.

But on the other hand, if you would like to assign the value of 3 to just the first level of the array and then add different numbers to the other levels, you would need to use the following code to make it happen:

Caulfield Lair (1) = 3

Working with strings and arrays are a good way to make sure that you are getting the code to work in the right way. The strings are going to be statements that happen inside the code and make it easier for you to write out the different things that you would like to have happen, either by adding in the whole string to the code or just having a few parts as you see fit. The arrays are going to be responsible for holding large pieces of data in a way that is easier to look through and reach inside the code. Both of these are going to be important to ensuring that you get more out of the code and that   it   works   the   way   that   you   want.

Chapter 4: Manipulating the Variable Amounts

Now at this point we are going to take some time to look at the different operators and variables that you are able to use inside of your code. So far at this point we have learned a bit about how to create a simple program. But there is a lot of manipulation that you are can do inside the code and operators are a great way to help you to do this. The operators inside of Fortran is going to be a great way to do mathematical functions while also getting these results to show up on the screen. With all that we have learned so far about this program, it is now possible to work on a short program on our own that will help to manipulate the amounts of variables. So basically inside of this chapter, we are going to learn how to make our program in Fortran do some basic math.

First we need to take a look at what the variable is all about. A variable is basically a little container that is going to store information inside of the memory of the computer. You are able to use these to hold either one or more value of your choice, and you are able to assign this either at the beginning of your block of code or when the code is being executed.

Assigning a variable is going to be pretty easy to accomplish. You will just need to use the (=) in order to pick the value that you would like to use along with the variable. You are able to add more than one value to the same variable if you would like to store them together in the code, but for the most part, it is just going to be one variable that you are working with. You can add in many different variables inside of the code, but the operators that we are going to talk about in a minute help to make it easier to get this all done.

Before we get too far into making this kind of program, we are going to take some time to work with operators. While these are pretty simple, there are some times when they can seem confusing and will make you wonder what they mean. The trick with these is to not think of them as mathematical symbols. For example, when it comes to writing out a = 2, you should see this as the value of 2 is going to be stored inside the memory of your computer that is labeled as a. Here is another example that you can use:

a = 2

b = 3

c = a + b

In the statement that we did above, you will see that the value of 2 is going to be stored as the memory location that is a and then you will see that the value of 3 is stored in the memory location that is called be. And then when you add the values of a and b together, you are going to store that result under the memory location of c. Keep in mind with this one that you are not able to write out this kind of equation as a + b = c because the compiler is going to see this as an error. The one variable needs to be on the left-hand side of your symbol and then you can have as many of the variables as you would like on the right-hand side, but mixing these around are going to cause an error message.

Arithmetic operators

Now that we have looked at some examples of operators, it is time to work with some of the operators that you need. Not all of the math symbols that you will need are going to show up on the keyboard, but the Fortran does have some of its own symbols that you are able to use in order to represent the different math operands that you are able to use. Some of the most common arithmetic operators that you are able to use on your language includes:

- (+): this is the one that you are going to use for addition
- (-): this is the one that you are going to use for subtraction in the code.
- (*): this is the one that you are going to use for multiplication
- (/): this is the one that you can use for division

One thing to note with these is that you can use more than one of the symbols, whether you are using three addition signs or an addition and a division symbol, inside the same part of code. You are able to use as many of these as you want, but you need to use the order of operands to do it. This means that you will need to do all of the multiplication, then the division, addition, and subtraction, going from left to right to make sure that the compiler is going to give you the right answer.

Other parts of your code

As a beginner, you will wonder what all the blanks, or the skip positions, are inside of the program. Some people choose to write out their programs without using these at all, but for the most part, the programmers like to include these inside of their code in order to make it easier to read. You are able to choose how you would like to use a skip position, but you should include at least a few to make sure that your code is easier to read through.

There are also some special characters that you are able to work with inside of your code. These are used in order to deliver the function that you want. These are going to seem pretty simple and plain but you need to be careful about how you use them. If you use them the wrong way or place two of them into the code right next to each other, you could end up with conditions that cancel each other. Some of the special characters that are found inside of Fortran and that you should watch out for include:

- (/): this one is going to specify another line
- ("): to output strings
- (:): this is going to terminate a list
- () this is going to categorize the descriptors.

Descriptors can be a tool that you are able to use and they are variables that are going to specify the amount of data that is required for a conversion. It is a good idea to keep track of the usage of these since the process may not end unless you add in the right descriptor is placed inside. Some of the descriptors that you can use include:

- A: repetition
- D: this one is for digits next to your decimal points.
- E: this is for an exponential number
- M: this is the minimum amount of digits.
- W: this is width in total characters.

You are going to be able to use all of these different parts to help you to get the code to work the way that you would like. You can mix and match a few of the parts to get the variable to be the right number, to store it in the right place inside the code and to do so much more. When you are able to add in the operators of the Fortran code, work with the blanks or the skip positions to make the code easier to use, and add in the special characters and the descriptors to the code, you are going to get a lot of power and options inside of the code.

Chapter 5: Working with Conditional Statements

At this point, we are going to take some time to look at the if statements. These are the most basic of the conditional statements and you will find that they are pretty straightforward. With this one, you will set the condition that needs to be met as well as the action that will show up at the same time with it. If the user puts in an input that matches, you will see that the program puts up the action that you choose. On the other hand, since this is a simple equation to work with, when the user puts in an input that is seen as false, the program is just going to end because you didn't set up an action.

So for this one, let's say that you just want people who are 18 to be able to get into the website. You would set up the if statement to accept any answer that is 18 and above. If the user places their age inside to be 20, the action (such a statement that you choose) will be executed by the compiler. But if the user puts in that their age is 16, then the program is going to see that this answer is false compared to the conditions that you set, and since you are using the if statement, nothing is going to happen.

Now there are some issues that can come up with this, but let's just focus on learning the syntax and getting this part down. Take a look at the syntax below for this:

if (x == 1) then

print *, 'turn left'

end if

The logical operator is the one that is used in this example along with the statement of if..then..end if. Note the expression that comes after the if statement. It is going to provide you with a test, something that is necessary when you are trying to imply a condition. In this case, we are going to assume that the "x" variable is an integer. One of the values that it can be is equal to 1. Interpreting this as a logical operation, the program is going to test to see if the value of the variable is 1. Then it will check if this is true or not. If your variable is 1, then the statements that come next will be executed which in this case would be the words "turn left". Then the end if is going to terminate the program that you are working on.

The if...else statements

As we mentioned in the last part, the if statement is going to be pretty basic
and there are some issues with it. Your user may very well be 16 years old
and it isn't a good idea to have the program just end if they put in this
answer. You most likely will want to have some message come up at least,
so that the user doesn't assume that something is wrong with the program.
For example, if they put that their age is over 18, you would want to set it
up to say something like "Welcome to the site!" and then have the next
action be that they can get in. But if they put in that they are 16 or
something else, you would rather have a message like "Only those over 18
are allowed in the game!" than having the program just end.

The if...else statement is able to help you to do that. You would set it up like
the first part that we had above, but then you would add the else that
catches anything that is considered false by the compiler based on the
conditions that you set. This allows you to have an answer, any answer,
come up regardless of what input the user is giving to you. This makes it
much more clean cut and easier to deal with and doesn't leave the user
wondering what is wrong with the user.

In addition, you are able to make it so that there are several options that
come up. Let's say that you would like to have someone pick out their
favorite color of either red, green, yellow, or blue. You would just need to
write out more of the else sections of this code would just keep going.
Another really useful thing for you to learn how to use inside of your
Fortran code is the conditional statement. These are really great because
they allow you to have some extra power and choices inside of the code.
These will allow you to put in the conditions that need to be met in order to
get different statements or actions to occur. They can be really simple, such
as the if statement, where you will only have an action happen when the
answer is inputted is true compared to your conditions, you can have it so
that a different action will happen based on if the answer is true or false
based on your condition, or you can give the user some choices.

You can decide what conditions need to be met before you allow the user to
put in their information. This allows the code to keep things simple and it
can look at your conditions before executing what you would like to have
happen. You can make these as complex or as simple as you would like, but
remember that you do need to base these on Boolean expressions. You

have to leave the answer as either true or false based on the conditions that you set.

Don't worry if this sounds complicated right now. We are going to take some time to look over the different conditional statements that you are able to work with and help you to get the results that you want, no matter what kind of conditional statement you are working with.

The if statements

down the line, taking a look through each condition and statement that you put onto the screen. You can also add in a catch or break at the end so if the user picks pink or another color that isn't listed there so they still get an answer.

There are so many options that you are able to do with the if...else statements and they can really open up a lot of what you are able to do inside of your code. You can make them as simple or as complex as you would like, adding in more sections or just having a true and false option. Mess around with this a bit and see what you are able to come up with on your if...else statements.

Conclusion

Working in a coding language can be difficult no matter who you are. Many beginners are worried that they are not going to be able to find the answers to getting started or that it is just going to be too hard for them to pick out how to work with this code. But when it comes to working in Fortran, you will find that writing out a code can be nice and simple and it won't take that long for you to learn it and start working on your own.

This guidebook is going to take some time to help you learn how to work with the Fortran code. We are going to start out with writing some of our own codes while learning about some of the basics that come with Fortran. We will then move on to working with strings and arrays, understanding how the loops work, and even working with conditional statements. These are actually really important parts of working with a coding language, but since Fortran is so simple to work with that you will be able to add them into a code in no time.

When you are ready to get started on writing some of your own codes and want to get into the world of coding, working with Fortran is one of the best options to help you to get this all done. It is an older language that is meant for beginners and you will be able to catch on to it in no time at all. Use this guidebook to learn what you need to know in order to get the Fortran language to work for you.

Book 2

XML

By: PG WIZARD BOOKS

Step by Step Guide To Mastering XML
Programming!

XML Crash Course: Step by Step Guide To Mastering XML Programming!

Table of Contents

Introduction

When it comes to getting into the world of coding and all the programming that you would like to do, there are many options that you are able to choose from. Some choose to work with options like Java and HTML so that they can create projects online and on web pages that really wow. Others like to go with Python because it is an easy one for beginners to work with. But a great coding language that you can learn to work with and which we are going to discuss inside this guidebook, is the XML coding language.

You will notice as you go through this guidebook that there are some similarities that come up between the XML language and the HTML language. While both of these are similar, there are some differences that come up and we will talk about these inside of this guidebook. We will also spend some time talking about some of the basics of XML, some of the parts that you would want to add into the code to make things easier, how to declare XML documents (which is something optional you are able to do to make the code work a bit better) and even how to work with the different character entities to help make coding easier. These are just a few of the things that we will discuss in order to get you familiar with the XML code so that you can use it on your own.

When you are ready to get started on a new coding language and you want to pick one of the very best that is also easy for beginners to work with, you should learn how to use XML. This guidebook is going to give you the best results to ensure that you will learn everything that you need to know in order to start with the XML language.

Chapter 1: What is XML Programming?

When it comes to learning a new programming language, there are so many choices and it can all seem a bit overwhelming. You want to make sure that you are picking choices that will get you ahead and will make it easier to work on the systems and programs that you want, but with all of the choices that are out there, how are you going to be able to choose the one that is right for you. There are choices for beginners and ones for those who want to be a bit more advanced. There are choices that are great for working on websites while others are good for a specific operating system or for working inside of your business statistics. There really isn't a right or wrong answer, you just need to take the time to look at the different options and find the one that is right for you.

In this guidebook, we are going to take a look at the XML program. This one stands for Extensible Markup Language and it is one of the most talked about programming languages, only second to Java, because of all the great things that you are able to work with. inside of this language, you are able to store, organize, and identify your information with the help of tags. If you have used Java or JavaScript programming in the past, you may have heard about HTML tags, but these two are not quite the same. The XML language is not one that is going to replace HTML later on down the road, but it does introduce some new possibilities because it uses some of the features of HTML.

So, to make this easy, the XML program is going to be software and hardware independent and it is often used in order to carry information. even though the markup that is used will look similar to what you are finding with HTML, you will see that these are two different entities. For example, XML is set up to focus on the data that you are using while HTML is more focused on the appearance of your data. XML is going to describe your data while the HTML is going to display the data when you are done.

To make this work better, let's take a look at a good example of how this will work. Keep in mind that you will need to define some of your own tags because these are not predefined inside of XML. Here is the example:

```
<note>
```

```
<to>Jane</to>

<from<John</from>

<heading>Memo</heading>
```
<body>Come to the meeting at ten in the morning tomorrow</body>

</note>

With this example, you are probably able to tell what is going on. The information is there for both the sender as well as the receiver and there are headings and a body message that you will be able to use. But remember that the XML document is basically going to contain the information that you want along with some tags. There are no specific functions that go with it. On its own, XML is going to be pretty useless until you get the right software program in there to turn it into something.

Now basically, you are going to have three characteristics that come with the XML language that you are able to use and you can remember these by thinking about the name of the program. The three characteristics that you can work with include:

Extensible: this means that the XML program is going to allow you the change to characterize your own tags so that they will work with your application. You will also be able to extend the concept of the document, which is usually a file that is going to live on the server. It can also be a piece of data that is temporary and will flow between the various web servers.

Markup: this it eh elements or the tags that are familiar inside of XML. The elements that you are creating in this language will be similar to the ones in HTML, but you will be able to define the elements or tags that you want.

Language: the languages that are used inside of HTML and XML are pretty similar, but there is some more flexibility when using XML. You are able to use it to create and define some other languages rather than just having it set in stone like HTML.

Do I really need to learn how to use XML?

XML Crash Course: Step by Step Guide To Mastering XML Programming!

Many people wonder if it is worth their time to learn how to use XML since it is so similar to what you will find in HTML. You do need XML because there are times when you would like to create and deal with the data. The HTML document is just going to display the information; it is not going to work with it to make it look nicer or anything else.

In addition, working with XML allows you to use different contexts that are not just found on the web, including applications and web services. Any time that you would like to organize your data and send it over to another person, without having to worry about all the displays like you would find with HTML, the XML language is going to be the one to work with.

Downloading the XML language

Before we go any further in this guidebook and learn how to write some codes (as well as some of the other cool things that you are able to do in this language), we are going to need to take some time to get all of this downloaded onto the computer. The XML language is from Microsoft and at the time of this book, the XML Parser 3.0 is the option that we are going to use for our projects.

First, you need to make sure that the operating system and computer are the right kind to run this. To work with the XML Parser 3.0, you will need to have a Windows computer that is Windows 2000, Windows Server 2003, or Windows XP. You can then go to the Microsoft website to find this version, or a newer version, of the XML program an download it to your computer. Read through the prompts that come up on your screen until you get don with the download and it is all installed on your computer. At this point, you are ready to get started with some coding!

Chapter 2: Learning the Basic Syntax of XML

Now that we have the right program on our computer and ready to go, it is time to learn a bit about the syntax of a code in XML. If you learn the basic syntax of your code, it is going to be much easier to write more complex codes later on. Of course, with the options that we are going to talk about in this chapter, we are going to keep things pretty simple to start, but as you learn more about XML, it is pretty easy to add in the other parts that you will want to learn.

Below we are going to write out a basic syntax that you are able to use in this language and then we will take some time to discuss the different parts so that is makes sense for what you are doing. Here is the basic syntax that you can use:

```
<?xmlersio=”1.0^)>

<contact-info>

<name>Manny Dunphy</name>

<company>Real Realtor</company>

<phone>(895) 444-1111</phone>

</contact-info>
```

As you can see with this example there are several parts of information that are placed inside. You need to make sure that the right syntax is used and the right symbols, so that the compiler has an idea of what you would like to send. This is a pretty simple option that will have the contact information for this person, Manny Dunphy, who works with Real Realtor as well as their phone number. You can expand this out as much as you would like or keep it this simple.

Remember than when working in XML, we are concentrating on the data, and collecting the data, rather than worrying about how the data is going to look. If you plan on putting this kind of information into a website or you want to make sure that it looks nice, you are going to need to work with the HTML format to make this happen.

XML Crash Course: Step by Step Guide To Mastering XML Programming!

Working with XML declarations

When it comes to XML, there are some documents that are going to have declarations and some that will not. If your document is one of them that has the declaration, here is a good example of how you would want to write it all out:

```
<?xmlv version="1.0" encoding="UTF-8"?>
```

For this one, the version is going to be the XML version and the other specific encoding is going to tell the document that you are going to use character encoding for this particular project. As we go through some of the other parts that you are able to work on in this book, you will see some more of the XML declaration and it is going to make a bit more sense to you.

Tags and Elements

Next on the list to work with are the elements and tags. The elements inside of XML are basically going to be the building blocks. They are going to be like a container that will hold many of the different parts of the XML ode, including media objects, attributes, elements, and text. Pretty much any element that comes into the code could be placed into the containers here. Each document is going to contain at least one element, but often there will be more if the code is longer. You can use the scopes in order to delimit using a start or end tag. Here is a good example of how you would write out the syntax for the elements and tags:

```
<element-name attribute1 attribute2>

...content

</element-name>
```

The element name in this example is the name that you would give to the element in this place. The name needs to be the same and matching in the beginning as well as in the ending tags. The attribute1 and attribute 2 are the element attributes that are going to be separated by some white space. You will be able to use the attributes in order to refer to a property of the element and often it is going to be associated with not only a name inside the code, but also with a certain value that you assign.

Writing out a comment inside of XML

There are times when you would like to leave a little comment inside of the code. When it comes to coding, the comments are just messages that the compiler is going to skip over and not read, but which can be useful to you or the other programmers who would like to go through the code. You will find that the syntax for writing out comments inside of XML is going to be the same as doing so in HTML. You will be able to use this syntax in order to write out your comment:

<!—An example of a comment→

Comments will need to all be done in this manner to tell the compiler when to start and stop the comment. When the compiler sees this, it will just skip over to the next part of the code, without causing any delays or issues in the code. You are able to add in as many of these comments as you would like or feel that you need in the code to make things easier, but you should be careful to not add in too many or you will end up with a messy code.

Starting a new line inside of XML

There are times when you will want to get started on a new line in XML. When it comes to doing this in applications of Windows, the new line is going to be done with the carriage return and line feed. On the old MAC systems, the new line is going to be with the carriage return and in Unix it is going to be the line feed. But when you are using XML, this is all going to be done with the line feed. You are able to start a new line in the code when you need to keep things in order and to make it easier to read through the code.

Unlike what you are going to find with HTML, the XML code is going to see white spaces a bit different. While you are able to have several whitespaces in a row on HTML, you will not have this inside of XML. Instead, if you have more than one whitespace in a row, the XML program is going to take these and turn them into just one.

XML Crash Course: Step by Step Guide To Mastering XML Programming!

These are just some of the basics that you are able to use when it comes to working in the XML coding language. They are going to help you to form some of the basics of your code and can come in use later on when you are ready to write out some more complicated codes. Make sure to learn some of these basics to make it easier for code writing later on and to further understand how the XML code will work for you.

Chapter 3: Declaring Inside of XML

We discussed the XML declaration a bit earlier on, but now we are going to break this down a bit in order to help it make more sense for you to use. The XML declaration is going consist of the details that you need to put in order by an XML processor to break down and analyze the document of XML. This is an optional feature that you can choose to either use or not use, however, when you do choose to use it, you will notice that it occurs right at the beginning of the document. Here is the syntax that you can use for XML declaration to make things a bit easier to use.

```
<?xml

        Version="version_nmuber"

        Encoding="encoding_delcaration"

        Standalone="standalone_status"

?>
```

Each of the parameters that you are going to use will have their own name so keep these in line and then an equal sign as well as a value. You are able to set up the numbers, rather than the quotes, to get the code to react in the way that you would like. There are a few rules that you will need to keep in mind when you are declaring inside of XML and these rules include the following:

- If there is a declaration inside of XML, you will need to make sure that you position it as the first line in your document. If you put it somewhere else inside of the document, you are going to run into some issues.
- When working with a declaration inside of XML, you will need to have a version number attribute to help make it work.
- The names and the parameter values that you set are going to be case sensitive, and it is recommended that while working inside of XML you keep the names in the lower case.
- There is a proper order that you are going to use with the parameter name to ensure that the compiler will read it properly. The proper order includes

version, encoding, and then standalone, just like you will see with the example that we gave above.

- You get to choose the quote type that you use, either the single or the double quotes. Just make sure that this stays consistent in the code.
- You will also notice that in this declaration, you will not need to have a closing tag like you do in some of the other coding that you will work with.
- If you are doing an encoding declaration, this is going to be a bit different, but for the rest of the declaration, you will need to keep it all in lower case letters.
- If you find that there are attributes, entities, and elements that are referenced or defined by an external DTD, your standalone is going to equal "no".

So now that we know a few of the rules that go with XML declaration, let's take a look at how you would do this in the code to get a better feel for it. This example is going to have all of the parameters defined for us.

```
<?xml> version='1.0' encoding='iso-8859-1' standalone='no'?>
```

And that is all there is to declaring inside of XML. Any time that you would need to do this inside of your code, you can just use this simple syntax, and then add in the information that you would like inside. This makes it easy for you to get the results that you want and as you can see, this only takes up about a line of code (maybe a little more depending on the declaration that you are using) and then you are all set.

Chapter 4: Working with Character Entities and Comments in XML

We talked about comments and some of the characters that you would use in XML a little bit before, but now we need to take this a step further and start to work on how the comments and the characters are going to work when it is time to actually write the code that you would like. When it comes to working with comments inside of XML, you will notice that they are similar to the comments that you have in HTML. They are basically little notes that are added into the code that will help you and other programmers to understand what is going on in the code, but will have absolutely no effect on how the code will work when it runs. One thing to note when writing out a comment is that you shouldn't try to nest one comment inside of another, because this will just cause a mess and could bring up an error inside of the code. Here is an example of a code that would have a comment in it (take the time to write this in your compiler to get some good practice).

```
<?xml version="1.0" encoding="UTF-8"?>
<!—Test scores are uploaded by grade  →
<class_list>
        <student>
        <name>Lilly</name>
        <grade>B+</grade>
        </student>
        </class_list>
```

Of course, this is a pretty simple example that just has one student and it is likely that you would add in a few more to fill this out but it is a good look at how the comment would be able to work inside of the code. It explains that the test scores were going to be upgraded by the grade that you were using and since we only used one it was not the most important, but if you had a lot of other students in here, it would show up. Remember that you are able to add in as many of these comments as you would like, you just need to be careful about using the right symbols to tell the compiler what you are doing.

Character Entities

The entity of the XML document is going to be the root of the entity tree and it is really the starting point for the processor. It can also be seen as the placeholder. The entities are going to be acknowledged being in the document prolog or in the DTD and they will often work with symbols that are only used for the entities and never for the content inside the code. For example, the < and > symbols are only used for the closing and the opening and the character entities are going to be used to make these visible.

Types of character entities

There are a number of character entities that you will be able to use inside of your code including the following:

Predefined character entities

These character entities are going to be introduced in order to prevent the ambiguity that can come when certain symbols are used. For example, there could be some issues when the (<) and (>) symbols are used along with the angle tags of (<>). The character entities are going to help delimit tags. You are able to use some of the following tags in order to get the right results in your code without showing all of the ambiguity at the same time:

Greater than: &gt

Less than: &lt

Ampersand: &amp

Single quote: &apos

Double quote: &wuot

Numerical character entities

With this entity, we are going to use numbers in order to reference and define the character entity that we want to use. We are able to choose numbers that are in decimal and hexadecimal format. There are lots of numeric references that you are able to use, and sometimes there can be too many for you to remember. The numeric reference is a number that is found in the Unicode character set. The syntax that you are going to be able to use for the decimal number reference inside of XML includes:

&# decimal number.

And then when you would like to use the hexadecimal reference, you would go with the following syntax:

&#x Hexadecimal number

Named character references

Wile the numerical character entities are a great way to get started, remember all of these numbers can be really hard, especially as a beginner who is just getting started with coding. This is why most people are going to use the name character entity instead to make things a little easier. There are a number of different ways that you can name the actions that you want to do inside of your code with the name character references, but here are a few of the examples that you can try:

- Acute: this one is going to refer to a capital A character that will have an acute accent on it.
- Ugrave; this is the name of the small u that has a grave accent.

Character entities and types are important when it comes to working inside of your code. They are going to help you to give the assignments to your work, whether you choose to use the numeric or one of the other choices. You can pick out the one that is right for you to work on your XML code.

Chapter 5: Processing and Encoding Inside Your XML Document

In this chapter, we are going to spend some time working on processing and encoding inside of your document. When you choose to work with processing instructions, you are allowing the documents to contain instructions for every application. You should know that these processes and the instructions are not going to be included in the character data that we talked about in the previous chapter, but they will still need to be able to pass through the application that you are creating.

The processing instructions will allow you to pass on the information that you would like to all of the different applications. You are able to place these in any location of the document that you would like. In fact, you are also able to place them into the prolog, which could include the document type definition or DTD, or at the end of the document as the textual content. The syntax to use in order to make this happen includes:

```
<?target instructions?>
```

For this syntax, the target is going to be responsible for recognizing the application from which the instruction comes from. You will be able to place the name of any application that you would like to use to tell the program where the instructions are located to use. And then the part of the instructions is going to be used in order to describe any of the information that you would like the application to process in order to finish it out.

The processing instructions are not used all that often because of the specialties that come with it. But if you do choose to work with these processing instructions, you will use them in order to link your XML document to a style sheet. In order to make this happen, you would need to type out the following type of syntax:

```
<?xml-stylesheet href= "businessforms.css" type="text/css"?>
```

These are basically the instructions that your target application is going to process inside of the XML document. With this particular instruction, the browser is going to be able to get the browser to recognize the right target by initiating that XML document and that it should transform it before it is shown. Notice that the first attribute comes out as the type of XSL that you are trying to transform and then the second attribute is going to indicate the location of the type you are transforming.

Working with XML encoding

Now that we have talked a bit about using processing inside of the XML document, it is time to work on the encoding inside of your documents. The process of encoding inside of XML is to convert the Unicode characters that you are trying to use into binary ones. The moment that the processor for XML reads a specific document, it is going to immediately encode the document according to the encoding type that you pick to go with it. There are different types of coding that you are able to use and we are going to look at them a bit more below:

Types of encoding

Inside of the XML code, there are gong to be two types of encoding that you are able to use, the UTF-8 and UTF16. They can both be used in separate ways in the coding that you work on. But if you end up not picking out the encoding that you would like to use with your XML document, the default is going to be the UTF-8. The syntax that you are going to use will depend on the type of encoding that you are using. For the UTF-8, you would use the following syntax:

<?xml version="1.0" encoding="UTF-8" standalone="no"?>

And then the syntax that you would need to use for the UTF-16 encoding would include:

<?xml version="1.0" encoding="UTF-16" standalone="no"?>

As you can see, these are going to be pretty similar, you will just put in the different options that you are able to use for the encoding. You will just need to pick the one that is best for you or choose to leave it blank so that the UTF-8 is going to be picked by default. Here is a good example of using the encoding of UTF-8:

```
<?xml version=”1.0” encoding=”UTF-8” standalone=”no”?>

<contact-info>

        <name>Dunny Bobbins</name>

        <company>Real Realtors</company>

        <phone>(553) 512 1123</phone>

</contact-info>
```

With this example, we are using the UTF-8 encoding, as you are able to see by looking at that part of the code. This means that the 8-bit characters are the ones that you will use. For the most part, you would use this option when you want to have files that are encoded to be smaller because you are just going with 8 bits or smaller. If you don't care as much about the size of the file or you would like to get it to be bigger, the UTF-16 is going to be the option that you should use for your encoding.

And that is all there is to the encoding process. It is simple to use and will ensure that the document is going through the right processes to work properly. You can choose to go with either the UTF-8 or the UTF-16 based on your needs, but most of the time the UTF-8 is the best one to choose to go with and if you don't place an option into the code, you are going to find that the processor will choose to go with the UTF-8 by default.

Chapter 6: Working with the Elements and Tags

Earlier we spent some time talking about the elements and tags inside of the XML document, but we are going to now spend a bit more time on this to see how they actually work inside the code and how you can get them to work for your needs. When you are working inside of the XML program, tags are going to be one of the most vital parts. They are the foundation to your language because they are able to do so many things. You will be able to use them as a method to define the scopes of your elements, insert special instructions, declare settings necessary for parsing environments, and to insert comments. There are several different types of tags that you are able to use in XML and they are categorized by this:

Start tag

The start tag is the one that you will use in order to start all of the elements in XML that are non empty. You would be able to write it out similar to this: <address>

Empty tag

Another type of tag that you are going to use is an empty tag. In between the start tag and the end tag (which we are going to talk about soon), is the text that you are going to write out, or the content, of the code. If your element ends up not having any content, you will find that the tag is considered empty. There are a few ways that you are able to represent the empty elements that you are working with.

To start, if you would like to have an end tag that comes right after your start tag, you would just write it out like this "<hr> </hr>". You are also able to have an element tag that is completely empty such as writing out "<hr />". You are able to use these empty element tags for any of the elements inside of the code that aren't going to contain any content inside of them.

XML Crash Course: Step by Step Guide To Mastering XML Programming!

The end tag

In addition to the two types of tags that we have been discussing so far, you can also work with the end tag. This is just as necessary as working with the start tag because it tells the code when that particular part is all done or not. You would have a simple syntax to write out in order to make this happen, including </address>. This is going to be the complement to working with the start tag and you will need to have both of these in place inside of the code. Keep in mind that it will need to have the (/) symbol in front of it in order to prevent confusion and to help end out that part of the card.

Some of the rules for using tags in XML

Sometimes it can be a good idea to know the rules about the tags before you get too far into this process. This will help to speed things up and ensure that you are going to get the best results. Unlike some of the other languages that you will work with inside of coding, XML is going to be considered case sensitive. This basically means that you are going to have to take note and be careful when you are using upper case and lower case letters. The tags that you are creating inside of XML will need to be either all upper case letter or all lower case letters. You will find that a simple mistake in this field is going to give you some bad results, so always make sure to review each of the codes that you will use before finalizing them.

For example, if you typed into the code <address> and then ended it as </Address>, the code is going to have some troubles with these. The XML is going to see them as different because of the capitalization that comes with it, and it will start to treat this code as an erroneous syntax. In order to get this error fixed, you would have to change the ending tag so that it was lower case rather than the upper case that was used.

Another rule that you will need to keep track of when using your tags in XML is that you need to close them properly. For example, if you have a tag that is opened up inside of another element, you will need to make sure that it has been closed before the external element is all closed up.

When it comes to naming the tags that you will use, you need to be careful to get them the right way. For example, make sure that you are doing a good job of picking out the upper case and lower case letters and keeping them consistent when naming things is important. You also are not able to use any form of XML, regardless of the case that you are using, because it is going to confuse the processor and how it should behave. You can add in letters, digits, hyphens, underscores, and periods inside of the names of the elements. However, if you are using punctuation inside of this code, you are only able to use the underscore, hyphen, and period. The names of the elements are not able to have spaces. Outside of these simple rules, you are able to use any name that you would like to name the tags of your code.

Elements that are used in XML

Next on the list to explore are the elements that are inside of XML. The elements are kind of like the building blocks of the language, the part that is going to be built up on the foundation of the tags. These elements are great to work as containers that hold many things such as media objects, elements, attributes, and text and often they are going to hold many of these at once. Any of the documents that you work with inside of XML will have at least one of these elements, but the longer ones will hold more. For empty elements, the scopes will be delimited with the help of an empty element tag, but for the ones that have elements inside of them, the scopes are going to be delimited with the help of a start tag and an end tag.

Writing out the syntax of the element can be pretty easy, but here is a simple example to help you get it started:

<element-name attribute1 attribute2>

Whatever content you would like to add into here.

</element-name>

With the example above, the element name is going to be whatever name you would like to give the element in this case and then the attribute 1 and the attribute 2 are going to be the attributes that you give to your element, and they will be divided up with some white space. The attribute word is going to pretty much define the property of the element. It is going to work by associating the name back to the corresponding value, which is typically going to be a string of characters. When you would like to write out the attribute, you will simply write it out as name="value" and that is it.

When you are working on writing out the name of your element, take the time to see that the name you use in the start tag will be the same as the name that you place into the end tag. In addition, the word name should have an equal sign with it, as well as a string value that is inside of either double quotes or single quotes.

What about the empty element?

So above we were talking about a code that has an element inside of it. But there are times when you will have an empty element. Basically, the empty element is going to be an element that doesn't have content in it. When you are writing the syntax for this one, you would need to use the following format to tell the processor what to do:

If you are trying to create a new document and you will need to use a variety of elements, the following format is going to be the best:

<?xml version = "1.0"?>

<contact-information>

<address category = "home">

<name> Wendy Dawn </name>

<office> My Office </office>

<phone> (632) 246 1234 </phone>

<address/>

</contact-information>

XML Crash Course: Step by Step Guide To Mastering XML Programming!

Working with elements and tags inside of the XML document is one of the best things that you are able to do for your code. These are going to help you to get everything in place and they are the foundation and the building blocks that you really need inside of your code. It can take some time to learn the different things that you need inside of these, but when you are able to bring it all together, these are the two parts of the code that you need in order to really get it started the right way.

Chapter 7: Viewers and Editors in XML

Inside of XML, there are several methods that you are able to use in order to view documents. For example, you are able to use a browser in order to view a document, or you can choose to go with a simple text editor. Most of the browsers that are available will support XML, so this shouldn't be a worry. Or you can choose to just click on the files for XML and get them to open up; but remember that this is only going to work if the XML file is a local one. If the file is one that is found on your server, you just need to type in the right URL path into the address bar, just like when you want to open up some of the other files on your browser.

As mentioned, there are many ways that you are able to look and view the XML documents at any time that you would like and the method that you choose is going to be a personal decision. Some of the options include:

XML text editors: there are many text editors that you are able to use and you can make the decision that is right for you. Notepad, TextEdit, and Textpad are great options to work with to create and view documents in XML, but other options will work as well.

Google Chrome: while all browsers are going to work well with XML, this one is really good to work with. there seems to be few problems with using it and it makes it easy to open up the XML code you want to use.

Mozilla Firefox: this one is also a good browser to use, but you do need to first open the code in Google Chrome. To do this, you need to take the file and double click on it in order to see the code displayed in some colorful text. This is a good thing because it makes it easier to read the code. Then at the left portion of the element, you will see a plus and a minus sign. If you click on the plus sign, the code is going to expand but if you click on the minus sign, you will see that the code hides.

Errors in my document

There are times when there will be some errors in your XML documents. If you notice that the code is missing out on certain tags, there are some errors that are going to show up. If there is an error somewhere in the code, you are going to get a message that should contain some information about the error that you are

51

dealing with. sometimes it is something simple such as misspelling a word or using lower case in the start tag and then upper case in the end tag. You will need to double check your code to see what the issue is so that you can make some changes to the code.

Editors in XML

When you are working inside of XML, you are going to need to work with an editor of some sort. The editor is going to be useful to create, as well as make changes, in the document that you are using. There are many different editors that you are bale to use and most of them are free and may even come on your computer already, so this can make things easier. For example, Notepad or Wordpad are two great options that you can use, or you can download a professional editor to use from online. The online editors are a bit more powerful and sometimes beginners like to go with them because they do some of the work, such as close tags that you leave open, check the syntax, and highlight the syntax in color so that it is easier to read. You can make the decision about what kind you would like to use and the features that you think will be the most helpful when you are learning how to code.

Conclusion

Working with a new coding language is something that can take some time and effort. You want to be able to get the most out of the language, but you also don't want to waste your time on something that is too hard to learn and understand. This guidebook is going to take a bit of time to discuss the XML coding language, how to use it and why you would want to learn this particular language.

Inside this guidebook, you are going to learn everything you need in order to do well with the XML code. We are going to start out with some of the basics that come with XML coding, such as what it is and how it varies from HTML (even though both of them are pretty similar) and then move on to some of the special parts that are found inside of your first code so that you can become more familiar with it all. Then we move on how you would declare inside of XML (which is something that is optional and you can choose to do or not) along with working in comments and special characters' amount other topics.

There is so much that you are able to do with the XML code once you take the time to learn this code and what all you can do with it. When you are ready to get started in coding or you are looking for a new code that you can work with, make sure to take some time to look through this guidebook and get the most out of the XML code.